FROM
SURVIVING
TO
THRIVING

FROM
SURVIVING
TO
THRIVING

Classroom Accommodations
for Students on the Autism Spectrum

JONATHAN CHASE

OUT OF THE BUBBLE PUBLISHING
PORTLAND, OREGON

Out of the Bubble Publishing, Portland, OR 97222

Editing and design by Indigo Editing & Publications

ISBN: 978-0-9981444-0-5
LCCN: 2016915447

For my dad, the real writer of the family.

Contents

Acknowledgments

Thank you to all of my Kickstarter backers! I'm grateful to have so many wonderful people on my team, and I appreciate each and every one of you.

I am especially grateful for the support of Buggsi Patel, whose incredible generosity in the final hours of our campaign put us over the top.

These Kickstarter backers really stepped up to make this book a reality:

Adam Stopka	Jessica Page
Barbara Avila	Joni Sanborn
Bill Stafford	Joyce Bernheim
Brad Volchok	Katherine Linstrom
Carol Barer	Kristie Pretti-Frontczak
Cynthia Arnold	Kristina Reiner
David Gonzalez	Krystin Sawyer
Dave Kelley	Lauren Corder
David Karstens	Leigh Ann Chapman
Debra McLean	Linda Stirling
Denise Hefner	Lyn Chase (Thanks, Mom!)
E. Lear	Marci Hammel
Eliana August	Matt Takimoto
Jeff Cox	Maureen Graham
Jeff Weaver	Melanie Gilbert
Jenny Schoonbee	Michelle Ayers
Jeri Swatosh	Michelle Harper

Michelle Kuepker
Nancy Fries
Pauline Newman
Randall Huebner
Rebecca Runo
Robert Parish
Ruthie Prasil & the Green
Apple Project
Sabrina LaField
Sam Berrett

Sandra Dibler
Steve & Tricia Byrne
Steve Task
Steven Keiser
Svuvar Kjarrval
Thomas J. Tracy
Tobi Rates
Victoria Colling
William Tremaine
Winona Avila

I would also like to thank Barbara Avila, Marci Hammel, and Sue Bert for sharing their expertise in the world of educational supports; Linda Stirling for teaching me about the world of publishing; and the Autism Society of Oregon board members for all their encouragement. I thank my dear friends Maria Siler and Michelle Harper for their endless positivity and support, and Victor Wooten and his Bass/Nature Camp team for showing me that I have a voice. And thanks to my editor, Kristen Hall-Geisler; book designer, Vinnie Kinsella; and the Indigo team for all their work in turning a messy, chaotic manuscript into a real live book!

Introduction

Since 2008, I have been a speaker, advocate, and mentor to young adults on the autism spectrum. I've met countless families, professionals, and individuals on the spectrum in my travels and witnessed great successes as well as great challenges. Everywhere I go I see young people with potential, and it's often the smallest things holding them back. My passion is to help others understand these young people and see the world through their eyes.

I understand students on the spectrum because I was one. I was diagnosed with Asperger's Syndrome when I was fourteen and a freshman in high school. My experience in the public school system was incredibly negative; I suffered at the hands of bullies for many years, struggled to connect with teachers who could not understand me, and left school after my freshman year. I earned my GED when I turned eighteen. I felt not only hopeless but that the education system was hostile because I didn't fit in.

I became a professional musician at the age of sixteen and worked full time in the music industry as a bassist for over ten years, playing hundreds of concerts with dozens of different bands. I found my way back into the autism field in my midtwenties, and what started as a little volunteer work grew into a career. I now speak at conferences, train professionals in autism understanding, and work with young adults in a number of ways. Every summer since 2012, I have run a foam sword fighting class to teach teamwork to teens and young adults on the spectrum. In the colder months, my mentoring clients meet up for Dungeons & Dragons sessions.

The Challenge of the Classroom

The classroom can be a challenging place for people like us. It can be noisy, chaotic, unpredictable, and a source of anxiety from the multitude of sensory, social, and intellectual tasks. Many students struggle in general-education classrooms for reasons that have nothing to do with their intelligence or ability to complete the same tasks as their peers. Even great teachers sometimes toil to find the right balance between supporting those with special needs and managing their responsibility to the rest of their students. The inclusive classroom is also where we learn the most, both academically and socially.

I understand and respect the difficult situation today's teachers face. Advocates (like me) come in and ask for numerous changes for individual students, and each Individualized Education Program (IEP) requests that you change parts of your whole system for just one student. There are many books about autism and educational support, but they are often dense tomes filled with deep terminology and jargon that requires immense time to sift through. Every book, workshop, and training expects you to become an autism expert when your goal is to support everyone in your classroom, not to dive deep into the realm of sensory processing disorders.

This book will teach you just enough about autism to understand your students. It will provide targeted accommodations that will make not only their lives easier but yours as well. Each tool or system is designed to be easy to implement and flexible enough that you can adjust my concepts to your classroom and teaching style. I've looked at my own experiences as a student, as well as the experiences of those I work with today, to design practical accommodations that will make a real difference for your students on the spectrum. I've consulted with teachers and professionals to find not just the tools that work for students but the best way for them to work for educators. Even the best accommodation is useless if the teacher can't put it into action. I've seen far too many "best practice" manuals gathering dust on bookshelves.

Whether you are a veteran educator or just beginning your journey, you will be meeting students like me. Some of us come with thick files of documentation and detailed IEPs, while others (like me) don't have a label to explain why we don't quite fit in. All of us are different, and you will often meet two students with the same diagnosis who could not be less alike. Yet, as you will see later, there are common differences that all of us on the spectrum share and certain supports that are effective for many of us.

Making Changes in the Classroom

If we begin with the assumption that you will have students on the autism spectrum in your classroom, then it's not a question of whether or not you are going to need accommodations to support them—it's a question of when and how you will implement those accommodations. I believe it's much simpler, for you and for the student, to build these accommodations into your classroom from the start. If they exist for every student, then you never have to single out those with special needs, and if you use these systems every day, for every student, you won't have to change your system when you encounter a student on the autism spectrum or with other special needs. I often find that universal accommodations aimed at students on the spectrum actually benefit everyone in the classroom.

Yes, it does take some work to make changes to your classroom environment. But when things go wrong, it takes just as much time to figure out what went wrong and fix it, and it's a lot harder on the student (and you). I have seen the process on both sides: as a student in crisis and as a professional working to identify the problem and find a solution. In my experience, classrooms with proactive accommodations have fewer crises and improve the odds of success for the student.

For students on the spectrum, every day is a minefield. There are many traps waiting that can impact the student in numerous ways, from minor burdens that put them behind schedule or cause them to lose track of their assignments to major crises that can force the student into a meltdown or shutdown, rendering them unable to participate at all. Little things can turn into big things; sometimes it's hard to even tell what went wrong or that things are escalating until it's too late and you are dealing with a crisis. Fortunately, many of these traps can be disarmed, or you can guide your student away from them.

By diffusing a small "land mine," you can have a ripple effect and increase the student's odds of making it through the project, day, or year without major incidents or issues that need to be addressed with significant changes. Instead of every day being a minefield, you can look at every day as a series of small successes. Every time a student takes advantage of an accommodation or utilizes a tool you have implemented, it's a success for both of you. Whether it happens once a day or once a year, over time the cost of implementing systems early far outweighs the cost of changing your system in response to crisis.

Changes that Benefit Everyone

Many students on the spectrum will struggle with similar issues or have similar themes in the issues that challenge them. By being proactive, you not only prevent those issues from coming up, you also remove the challenge of making major changes after the class has already begun.

My vision is a classroom that works for everyone: the typical student, the teacher, *and* the student who, like me, is a bit different. This is not a fantasy, and it won't take years of study and thousands of pages to find. It starts right now, with the idea that every accommodation can be built into your daily classroom system. These supports never single out a student with special needs unless it is absolutely necessary and only do so in the least restrictive way possible. Your classroom environment will utilize these concepts every day for every student, making it easy and natural for you to use and modify them for students like me who need a little extra support.

By developing your classroom with these tools on day one, you will increase the odds that students on the spectrum will find success there, and you will have greater success in your ability to support and teach them. The best accommodations are invisible. You will know you have found success when you don't even have to think about them anymore.

Overview

In the next eleven chapters, I'll cover specific ways of addressing the needs of students on the spectrum as they often arise in the classroom. These chapters cover both big-picture concepts, from autistic processing differences to student perspective, and practical solutions, such as using a homework basket. You will find tips, ideas, and a mix of concepts and specific accommodations.

Each chapter includes bullet points to make implementation easy—and easy to find again later when you need a refresher. There is also a case study in each chapter to illustrate how these changes can make real differences for students on the spectrum.

The accommodations in this book are designed to work independently of one another; you can mix and match to fit your classroom and the needs of your students. Some ideas may work better for certain ages or grades, but they are adaptable to work for students of all ages and abilities. Whether you implement one accommodation or every recommendation in this book, make them your own and adjust them over time with feedback from your students.

Part I

Understanding Processing and Control

In the coming chapters I will describe specific accommodations and exactly how to implement them in your classroom. But before you begin making changes, it's important to understand why these systems work for students on the autism spectrum. My approach to accommodations begins with a clear picture of how autistic individuals tend to process information and the differences between their perspective and that of their peers. While every student is unique, you will see common challenges and differences in students on the spectrum. With a sense of how these students see things differently, and understanding some common processing differences, you can make your accommodations more effective and target the areas where students on the spectrum need the most support.

My accommodations also utilize methods that not only help the student thrive but teach valuable self-advocacy skills. Putting control into the hands of your students will not only provide them with self-advocacy experience, it will make the accommodations easier to manage for you and reduce many of the factors that cause accommodations to fail over time. A balanced accommodation will not be solely in the hands of the teacher; it will share the responsibility between the teacher and the student, with flexibility to adjust based on the student's ability.

The following section will explain both of these aspects, offering you a clear view of how autistic processing looks from the inside and concepts you can use to put control in your student's hands. These concepts can be applied to any accommodation or system and should be used not just with the tools in this book but as a method of evaluating and modifying any support or system.

Chapter 1

Processing

Before we can design supports for a student, we have to understand what they need and how they perceive the classroom. Supporting students on the autism spectrum is challenging because the spectrum is so broad and each individual can exhibit radically different behaviors that require different levels of support. The word "autism" can mean so much, and it can have radically different meaning for different students. Each student on the autism spectrum will have a unique set of strengths and challenges. How do we even begin to understand what autism means and how to support these students if they are all so different?

I looked at all the people I know across the spectrum and then inward at my own experience to answer this question. I found several common threads that run across the entire spectrum and reveal similarities among everyone I know with an autism diagnosis. I see common differences in how we both process and prioritize information, invisible processes that can be difficult to see from the outside. Understanding these differences and the ways they change an autistic student's perspective is crucial to supporting the student and implementing appropriate accommodations.

Information Overload

The human brain is constantly at work, taking in an unfathomable amount of information every second. This vast amount of data is organized, sorted, and filtered in ways that allow us to function and survive in the complex world we live in. Most of us don't spend our precious mental processing power considering the difference in temperature when standing near a window, the faint sound of a conversation in another room, or the cut of our shirtsleeves and the way they fold underneath our arms. Everyone has a portion of their brain that's constantly filtering through all that information and feeding us only the most important or relevant pieces as they are needed. Without that ability, even simple tasks would become overwhelming and unmanageable.

Imagine driving to work every day with a keen awareness of the texture of your steering wheel, every nick in the leather seat beneath you, and the changing resistance as your foot presses down on the pedal. You try to focus on the road, the other cars, checking your mirrors, and thinking about your destination, but your mind is simultaneously analyzing the physical space around you and considering every aspect of it. The simple, familiar act of driving would become stressful, taxing, and for some, impossible to manage. You can drive to work every day because your mind is not prioritizing all of that information as equal. You are aware of the sensory experience but not focused on it. The sensory experience is dulled as your brain puts your focus on the most important thing—driving the car—and devotes little energy to considering the cut and texture of your shirt.

One of the great challenges for most people with autism is their reduced ability to prioritize everything they are taking in. They may want to focus—and intellectually, they understand that it is expected of them—but their brain cannot suppress all the other channels to devote maximum processing power to the task at hand. This can be especially challenging for children who have not yet developed skills and experience to better manage their focus and ability to suppress distractions.

To better understand how students can get overwhelmed, think about how your computer functions. When you give it a single task, it works efficiently and effectively. If you open more programs and assign additional tasks, it will function more slowly and eventually shut down. A series of simple tasks may be easy to manage, but when you burden it with multiple complex programs, it will struggle to handle them all.

Our brains work in a similar way: we work best when focused and become increasingly less effective and efficient as we juggle more tasks. The inability to prioritize information and suppress unimportant data can put students on the spectrum at a disadvantage before they even begin their first assignment.

Tasks and Attention

As you lecture the class, most students are devoting the majority of their processing power to interpreting your words and lesson, as well as to giving it context and working to retain as much as they can. Very little of their mental power is spent analyzing their sensory experiences in the moment, contemplating what comes next, processing the previous lesson, or retaining some shred of a conversation that occurred earlier in the day. If they were to list, in order, all the tasks their brain is managing, it might look something like this:

1. Understanding the teacher's lesson
2. Taking notes and referring to the textbook or written material

3. Interpreting the teacher's body language and other social cues
4. Looking to other students to confirm that their priorities are correct
5. Recognizing that their shoelace is untied
6. Considering the squeak of the teacher's pen as they write on the whiteboard

Each item is less important than the last, and while the list could go on and on, the first few items consume the majority of the student's mental power and everything else occupies just the tiniest sliver of their awareness.

The autistic student's experience is far different, even as an intelligent and capable teen or young adult. As you lecture, the student has some of their focus on the lesson, but they are also processing a multitude of other items. Their list of priorities is not so clean and organized:

1a. *My left sock is twisted, and the seam is underneath my toes.*
1b. *The light is brighter in the corner of the room than in the center, and one fluorescent bulb is flickering slowly.*
1c. *The texture of my pencil grates on my nerves as it scrapes across my paper.*
1d. *What activity are we doing next? Am I prepared for it? What if I don't finish this assignment on time? Did the teacher tell us what will happen next?*
1e. *I'm trying to understand the teacher's lesson.*
2a. *The boy sitting in front of me keeps glancing at the girl beside him. I wonder what he's thinking and if it relates to the conversation I had with him yesterday afternoon.*
2b. *My desk isn't quite level, and the legs rock back and forth just an inch when I write.*

2c. *I need to take notes and refer to the textbook.*

2d. *I forgot to turn in yesterday's assignment—when will the teacher allow me to turn it in? Or is it too late?*

2e. *The teacher made eye contact with me. What does that mean? Should I say something? Am I supposed to say something? I was trying to pay attention. Now I wonder if I made a mistake!*

The autistic student may have a combination of relevant and irrelevant information all being processed at once, prioritized far differently than their peers' and with no context to recognize the difference. The student may be juggling social, sensory, emotional, and intellectual information all at the same time. No wonder they look distracted when you call upon them midlecture with a question!

Tuning Out to Tune In

Sometimes students on the spectrum appear disengaged and "tuned out" from a lesson or lecture, but in fact they are shutting down "unimportant" processes such as maintaining eye contact or good posture to devote more mental power to interpreting the lesson. For most students, this is not a conscious effort but a necessary tool to survive in the complex, chaotic, overwhelming world they live in. It's instinctual. Some of us on the spectrum look away when someone is speaking, not because we are disinterested but because we are so focused on their words that we want to process and analyze each one at a very high level. By looking away we remove the responsibility of interpreting eye contact, body language, and a host of other social and visual cues. It simplifies the process and reduces the number of items we are trying to process at once.

Many of us on the spectrum begin a conversation with a mental priority list and item number one is "The words coming out of the other person's mouth." It makes sense to us, and as logical thinkers, that's where the important information should come from. However, that is not the case. Anyone in a conversation has to take into account eye contact, body language, tone, inflection, context, word choice, and many other social elements to deduce the proper meaning of those words. Our intention is to engage just like anyone else, but we don't have the innate ability to identify and filter out unimportant information.

I've worked hard to develop stronger social skills and integrate myself into social situations as a capable contributor. As an adult, I have put myself in challenging situations I could not have handled as a child and then analyzed both positive and negative outcomes. I made myself talk to new people, studied how they reacted to me, and invested considerable effort in cultivating and growing my social toolbox.

Despite all that work, there are three words that still challenge me, and I have seen them challenge my friends and clients as well: "How are you?" I didn't realize how tricky those words were or how easy it was to get them wrong until I was working at a temporary office job in my early twenties. I was the new guy on the floor, and a nameless coworker approached me in the hallway. He asked, "How are you?" as he passed by me without breaking stride. I began to answer his question, but he was already gone. Now what was I supposed to do? What the heck had just happened?!

Looking back, he was not asking me a question. "How are you?" really meant "Hello and goodbye." The words did not convey that meaning; the context and environment did. He assumed that I had the tools to interpret his meaning using all the available information and did not even consider that I could misinterpret his greeting.

"How are you?" is not just a greeting but a question that has different expectations based on many factors. I've heard those three words spoken with the same inflection and tone from a potential employer and from a dear friend I had not seen in quite some time. My friend does not expect me to say, "I'm fine," and leave it at that. At the same time, the potential employer doesn't really want to know how I am and probably won't hire me if I begin our conversation with a detailed description of my dog's bellyache that kept me up the night before and my worries about the cost of a trip to the vet.

"How are you?" shows that sometimes the words are the least important element of communication; this puts people like me, who are not very good at perceiving nonverbal cues, at a real disadvantage in social situations. Sometimes a student will blurt out something inappropriate or become hopelessly lost in a conversation. Other times they will answer very slowly, devoting all of their brainpower to navigating the social maze and checking their work before giving a careful and deliberate answer.

These difficulties in prioritization also contribute to the risk of becoming overwhelmed by options or unclear guidelines. When a child is presented with a dozen blocks on the floor and told to "put them back in the box," the obvious question is: Which one do I pick up first? Most children would select an arbitrary starting point, but an autistic child may become hopelessly overwhelmed by their inability to select a starting place and create an orderly list to follow.

What Do Balloons Do?

Some of our experiences are fundamentally different from our peers'. For example, for my entire life I've been afraid of balloons. Regular, harmless, birthday party balloons make me break into a sweat. As a child I would cover my ears or flee at the sight of even a single balloon. As an adult I've learned to control my reactions better, but my instinct is the same. Why would a grown man be afraid of balloons?

What do balloons do? They pop. When I experience a sudden, unexpected, loud noise, I experience physical pain. It's hard to describe, but it compares to being punched in the stomach. When I see a balloon I think, *It may not pop, and I may be just fine, but this thing could harm me, and if it does, I cannot anticipate it, prepare for it, or protect myself.* Looking at it that way, it's perfectly logical to be afraid.

Every person on the spectrum has a unique perspective and may experience certain situations differently than their peers. It may not be loud noises that are different for them—it may be touch, smell, a certain word or phrase; any experience has the potential to be processed differently. I don't choose to feel pain when a balloon pops. In fact, I wish I could turn it off and be done with the anxiety it brings. My experience is unique, as is my reaction to it.

The key is to recognize how fundamentally different the experience is and how hard it may be to see from the outside. If I didn't have the tools to articulate why I am afraid of balloons, I would be judged only by my reaction to them, which probably looks crazy or at least illogical. There may be times when you see a student react in ways that don't make sense to you or don't appear logical. Take a step back and consider that their perspective and experience may be different from yours, and from that of their peers. Maybe they have their own "balloon," and it will make perfect sense once you learn to see it through their eyes.

Understanding the student's perspective is the first step in designing effective accommodations. Any support has to start with a clear view through their eyes and account for the unique ways that students on the spectrum process information. But it's not the only factor to consider; if you focus only on the student's perspective, your systems may have unforeseen consequences, creating a new challenge for each one you solve. To create balanced, effective accommodations, you also have to consider how much control the student has in utilizing them.

Chapter 2

Control

The need for control is universal. People feel best when they're in control and have the ability to manage their own circumstances. Whether you are driving a car or having a discussion with your boss, you feel more anxiety and stress when you lose command of the situation.

The desire for control goes even deeper for many people on the spectrum, and it can be a powerful motivating factor; some of us feel the need to be in charge completely, all the time, without compromise. Each individual will have a different reaction when their sense of control is taken away, and many students on the spectrum will respond strongly with such reactions as:

- Appearing disengaged or disinterested
- Refusing to participate
- Shutting down
- Becoming increasingly upset
- Melting down

Students on the spectrum may use these reactions as a defense mechanism to avoid the unknown or situations where they may become vulnerable. Even small things can be upsetting to those who are hypersensitive, and small risks can appear quite dangerous to their eyes. Handing the reins to someone else can be frightening, especially if that person has the power to determine where you go, what you will do there, and how long you will have to stay.

When I evaluate any accommodation or support, I begin by assessing both the level of control the student actually has and how much they *feel* in control. These are two sides of the same coin, and sometimes the level of control the student thinks they have is more important than their actual power. The power comes from a sense of empowerment and the freedom to advocate, not from a false sense of authority. As you will learn, there are many ways to increase the student's control over their accommodations and to provide them with a greater sense of control within the classroom.

Giving the Student Agency

We can build control into supports in many ways and with many layers. For example, imagine a child who becomes upset or worried if they do not have the necessary supplies for class. They may even face anxiety over the fear that one day they will run out of supplies or be unable to find the supplies they need. You could develop a daily routine of checking to ensure that they have pens, pencils, and a fresh notebook to write in. Your goal is to help the student, but the accommodation has made them powerless. If you forget, even once, they may lose faith that you are trustworthy and will help them when they really need it. If they run out of paper or break a pencil, their only choice is to wait until you come to check on them and discover the issue. The student is completely reliant on you to assess and address their needs, and *you* are doing all the work!

The alternative is to empower the student by giving them tools to advocate for themselves as much as they are able, with your support coming as needed instead of acting as the sole provider of the accommodation. Here are a few options that address the same issue as above but put the power back into the student's hands:

- Create one location in the classroom with extra supplies and give *all* of your students clear instructions on when and how to access it. "Whenever you need a pencil or some paper, this drawer has extras and you are free to go and get what you need without asking." If you do this as a classroom rule instead of a disability-specific accommodation, you are supporting the student's ability to self-advocate just like their peers. You are removing a potential land mine while giving the student complete control over their needs.

- Create a classroom rule that everyone should be willing to share if another classmate needs something. Teach the students that they can ask anyone for assistance and have faith that a fellow student will assist them. As in the last example, this empowers the student on the spectrum without singling them out.

- Assign a "buddy" or partner who the student can go to for help with supplies. Seat a friendly and flexible student nearby and give them some guidance so they are prepared when the student on the spectrum needs help. Tell the student on the spectrum, "Jenny sits at the desk next to yours and she always has extra paper and pencils. You can ask her anytime you need some, and she will help you out." Again, you are empowering the student with total control and letting them evaluate their own needs and decide when to act.

Any of these supports can be followed up with some individual guidance. If a student does not have the communication or advocacy skills to take total control, you can still find ways to support them in a partnership.

Here are a few examples of supports for students who need the same support managing their school supplies but require additional assistance:

- Arrange a regular check-in time to go over supplies with the student and let them know that they can come to you at any time if they run low before your scheduled check-in.
- Give them a cue or reminder that alerts them when supplies are low. For example, place a colored sheet of paper near the bottom of the stack, which gives a visual reminder when they are almost out.
- Have a teacher or aide assist them as they normally would, but give the student one specific area where they have additional responsibility. For example, have the aide monitor the student's supplies, but give the student specific directions that if they need extra colored pencils, they should let the aide know and ask for help. The specifics are secondary to the concept: give the student some responsibility and control, even if it's minor.

The Pitfalls of Removing Control

When we support someone on the spectrum, we often remove all of their control in an attempt to make things easier on them. I've seen parents who, after learning what their child likes to eat, buy the same items every week, even past the age when the child could learn to request them and learn to help with the shopping list.

The parent is trying to make life easier, but the result can stunt the child's ability to self-advocate. Instead, as the child matures, the parents could increase the child's responsibility in tracking what needs to go on the grocery list and even "forget" to resupply from time to time, forcing the child to evaluate and advocate.

It's easy to take away someone's control in an attempt to support them or make things easier. For example, a student has a verbal altercation with a classmate and they are clearly dwelling on it or still affected by it the following day. You approach the student at lunchtime and say, "Hey, what happened with Jenny yesterday? Can you tell me what went on between you two? I want to help, but you need to give me some information." While you are trying to help the student and find ways to support them, you have taken away their control:

- They must talk with you now. They have no control over *when* the conversation will take place.
- They must talk with you here. They have no control over *where* the conversation will take place.
- The conversation must be about the topic you have presented. They have no control over what will be discussed.
- They must give you this information through verbal conversation. They have no control over the method of communication.
- You have set expectations for the conversation and outcome. They have had no time to prepare, process, consider what they want to share, or set their own expectations and ideal outcomes.

The student is then faced with a choice: participate and have no control, or refuse to participate and have 100 percent control.

Even if it is not in their best interest, some students will refuse or disengage rather than accept the burden of doing everything on your terms.

Clearly there has to be a discussion about the issue with Jenny, and you are responsible for getting to the bottom of it. There are many layers of control that you can concede to the student without abandoning your goal, such as:

- Invite the student to talk and ask them when they would like to discuss it. You could give several options, such as before lunch, after lunch, or tomorrow morning. You can also give a time range, and say, "How about you come to me anytime between now and Friday, and we'll talk about it?" There is still a boundary there to ensure the issue is addressed, but now the student can dictate the timeline and prepare for it.

- Allow the student to select the location. "Should we talk in the classroom, the office, the library, or out in the hallway?" Of course it makes no difference to you, but it can be a major control element from the student's perspective. How often do you get to tell your teacher where to go?

- Offer alternative methods to describe the incident. Could the student draw it, write a letter, or have a friend join to act out the scene? Even if they refuse, just giving them the option says, "We are partners, and you have some say in how we do this."

- Ask the student to think about their ideal outcomes. What would they like to get out of this? Do they have any ideas for a solution? This is more effective when giving them time to prepare rather than having the conversation right then.

- Ask the student if they would like Jenny, or a friend or witness, to join as well. Chances are they will decline, but they might just surprise you, and making the offer shows flexibility and your willingness to do things their way.

Ceding Real Control to the Student

Adding layers of control can reduce the student's anxiety, increase their willingness to participate, and teach self-advocacy skills all at the same time. When you look at a possible task or issue, ask yourself:

- Where can I give the student control?
- What are the areas that I absolutely cannot concede?
- Are there any ways to give the student control in a way that does not impact the outcome or my ability to take action?
- Does the student feel that they have control? How much? Do they feel forced, pressured, or cornered?
- Does the student have the opportunity to provide input and advocate for their own preferences?

I am not advocating for misleading the student or creating the illusion of control. A magician can force a spectator to pick the ace of spades every time, and it looks like free choice from the outside, but the spectator's belief is founded on a lie. In the same way, a student can be presented with meaningless options, inconsequential decisions, or asked for feedback that serves no purpose save the idea of engagement. That being said, it is possible to offer the student additional options that give them a greater range for choosing how to react to your request.

For example, give them the option to type a letter, write it by hand, or dictate it to an aide or classmate. The medium doesn't change your ability to act on the information they provide, but it gives the student a sense of control and empowerment to impact their situation in the way that feels best to them. If the student opts to write a letter by hand, give them a selection of pencils, colored pens, or any other writing tool they prefer. Their choice to write about Jenny in green pencil instead of black ink is inconsequential to you, but some students will see that as a major victory and the opportunity to do things in their own way.

Choice and Control

Choice and control can mean the same thing in many areas, and simply asking a question will make the student feel more at ease. When I was in middle school, I had issues accessing my locker and toting all my books and supplies from class to class. I would either forgo the trip to my locker and arrive to class without my textbook, or I would trek to my locker, struggle to get it open, and arrive to class equipped but late and very stressed about it. How different would my experience have been if a teacher had asked, "Would you like to keep your textbook on the shelf in here so you don't have to fetch it out of your locker every day?" It would have removed a huge burden and stressor in my daily routine, and I would have felt a greater level of trust with that teacher. The fact that they asked me—instead of saying, "This is how we are going to do things: from now on I am keeping your textbook after class; don't take it to your locker anymore"—would have shown empathy and interest. The question has to be genuine, but sometimes students will surprise you, and the only way to learn is by asking the question. Had my teacher asked about the accommodation of leaving the book on the shelf, they could have even followed up with "Or do you have another idea about how to make this easier?"

The issue is the same for a student today: they can't manage the time and physical burden of going to their locker between classes to get a textbook. There are two ways to approach the student about it:

- "I'm going to keep your textbook on the shelf in here. Take it down every day when you come to class and put it back on the shelf, not in your locker, when the bell rings."
- "I noticed that sometimes you forget your book and you seem pretty stressed when you are coming in late with it. What would you think of leaving it here instead so you don't have to walk all the way to your locker before class? Would that help? Or do you have any other ideas on how we can make this a little easier on you? If you want to think about it and talk about it later in the week, that's okay too. Just let me know when you are ready, okay?"

The first conversation is one-sided, and the student may refuse simply to avoid being "bossed around" by the teacher. Looking back, I know that I had many encounters with teachers where I refused support simply to remain in control, even if that control came through as defiance. The second conversation addresses the same issue, and you may go into it feeling pretty sure that the student is going to accept your proposal. The difference is that they have options and input.

If the student declines and continues to struggle, then it may be time to reframe the issue by saying, "Let's just give this a try for a week, and if it is not easier after a week, then we'll meet up and talk about it again." It takes away a layer of their control but still gives the student an opportunity to advocate for themselves.

Control is a not a box to check or one specific modification to add to your system. It's a constant evaluation of the student's role and responsibility within each accommodation and system developed to support them. Ask yourself if the student has options, choices, and genuine feedback in the process. Does the support work with them, or for them? Are the choices presented to them matched to their individual needs and flexible enough to evolve as the student matures?

The following chapters will detail specific accommodations and share many ways to incorporate control and options while keeping the student involved and engaged. But the concept of control is not limited to the systems detailed in this book; it's an open-ended approach with the goal of building an alliance with your student. Once you understand the student's perspective and provide the student with options that fit their way of thinking, your alliance will grow stronger, the student will buy into the things you offer, and every accommodation will be more successful.

Part II

Classroom Accommodations

The following chapters will offer specific accommodations, tools, and concepts to apply to your classroom. These can be mixed and matched in any combination and adjusted to meet the needs of individual students.

Overall, the goal is to provide a classroom environment with structure, rules, and options that benefit most students on the spectrum. Each accommodation is designed to be proactive and eliminate issues before they occur or reduce the likelihood that certain common challenges turn into crisis situations.

Change and transition can be difficult for individuals on the spectrum, and it is much easier to begin with a set of rules and expectations, which are explained on day one, than to wait until a crisis happens and then implement sweeping changes.

Remember to be flexible and creative and to invite input from your students. You may be surprised by their ability to advocate, problem solve, and offer creative solutions when given the chance. Also remember that, regardless of their diagnosis, every student grows and matures over time. Just because something didn't work in September doesn't mean it won't work in May.

Chapter 3

Clear Instructions

Black-and-white thinking is a common theme in the autism world, but it can manifest itself in many different ways. Logical thinkers like me want to break things down into categories, lists, labels, and clear plans. We want each task to have a step one, a step two, and eventually a final step, upon which the job is finished. A task that does not meet these simple criteria can become a great challenge; even identifying the first step to take may be a barrier to beginning the task at all.

Understanding black-and-white thinking begins by looking at phrases that are open to interpretation or are not meant to be taken literally. Even simple directions can lead to questions that are unanswerable, which leaves some students stuck and unable to move forward.

- "Everyone needs to finish their art project and get ready for gym class." *How do I know when my art project is finished? What steps does one take to "get ready" for gym class, especially if I don't even know what activities we will engage in when we get there?*

- "Shoot the basketball a few more times and then line up at either end of the gym." *How many times is "a few"? How do I decide which end to line up at? Does it matter whether I am at the front or back of the line?*
- "You need to finish up so we can go to the next class." *How do I know when I am finished? What if I don't feel finished? Can I come back to the project later? What does "finish up" really mean?*
- "Put your eyes on me." *Does the teacher want my eyes physically on top of her? How could I even do that?*
- "Clean up your desk area and get ready to go home." *How clean is clean? Am I supposed to wipe it down or remove old stains and pencil marks? What if my desk is old and scarred—how can I make it look clean? How exactly do you get ready to go home?*
- "Get out!" (Spoken sarcastically.) *I guess she wants me to leave the classroom. How will I know when it's time to come back?*
- "Turn around and sit down." *Okay, this one I understand. (Student spins around in a circle before sitting down on the floor.)*

A project with too many parts or choices can also become a problem because there is no clearly defined first step. Open-ended projects such as "Get some art supplies, take them back to your desk, and make a sailboat" are baffling and may overwhelm a student who needs their priorities set in an orderly manner. Which supplies do I need, and what is the *first* step in turning a sheet of colored paper into a sailboat? Some students may even wonder if they need a three-dimensional sailboat, a literal sailboat, or a photo of a sailboat so they can analyze its shapes and angles before cutting paper to create a two-dimensional representation.

Long-Term and Multipart Projects

I often struggled with long-term projects if the steps weren't laid out clearly. I was fine if the teacher gave me a plan: "First, research the subject through these sources, then take notes. Next, develop an outline and review the outline with a peer. Then craft that outline into a report and put it into a notebook. Here is the schedule for each step, and the final report is due two weeks from Friday." If instead the teacher said, "Write a report on this subject; it's due in a few weeks." I would have no idea where to start, what the process was, or how long each step would take. I might read up on the subject every day for weeks and then scribble out some notes on the last day, or read a single page about the subject and spend weeks trying to stretch my knowledge into a large document. Without clear instructions and a logical process, I had to guess, and my guesses were often incorrect.

Obviously, you cannot present every task in a carefully laid out list of instructions, but understanding how the student thinks, and where they might get stuck, can help you identify projects that need more instruction or take steps to prevent them from misunderstanding you.

Some people say that children on the spectrum often think like engineers or scientists. In some ways it's true: we want data, evidence, a timeline, benchmarks, and a clear plan that is obvious before we even begin. This doesn't always relate to intelligence or advanced academics—sometimes it's as simple as when you tell a child to "clean up these toys" and the child gets stuck trying to decide which one to pick up first. Another child may wonder if "clean" means to wash each individual toy in the sink. Rephrasing the direction to be: "Put the blocks in the box, put the box on the shelf, and then start putting the books back on the bookshelf," gives clear direction and a starting point, which eliminates many of the areas where children can become stuck.

Analyzing potential sticking points can start with giving a clear beginning and end. For most tasks it's as simple as starting at the top of the page and finishing at the bottom, but for tasks that are more open ended, you may need to offer recognizable boundaries. Writing tasks can have a word, page, or paragraph count. Art projects can have a visual such as "color half the page" or a time-based limit. Multipart projects, such as writing a report and then building a diorama to go with it, may require instructions that have a timeline for each phase.

It's also important to carry those boundaries through from one project to another. If a student is struggling to get started, even with a clearly defined task, it may be because they are still processing the end of the last project or they are perseverating on the next phase or end of the new project, which keeps them from focusing on the first step.

I've known some teens who become paralyzed when forced to make a decision, even if they are fully capable of the project itself. Telling them to "pick any state you want to write about" or "decide whether to write about Rome or Greece" puts them in a position which goes against their "scientist" mentality: making a decision without enough data, a clear right and wrong answer, or a clear understanding of the risks and consequences. In these cases it can help to talk with the student one-on-one to walk through the options and help them decide, or in some cases to remove the choice entirely (if it really doesn't matter and is just an issue of preference), to allow them to move on without having to make it.

Sometimes it's as simple as explaining why you are offering them a choice to begin with. They may believe that picking the wrong state to write about can result in failure and that the question itself is part of the test. You may be surprised at the places our minds will go if we are left to imagine the reasons for a task instead of hearing them explicitly from the teacher.

Arnold's Story

Arnold is in the eighth grade and has acceptable grades in every class except for art. Sometimes he turns in assignments that are not complete, and sometimes he spends far too much time completing other projects even after the class has moved on. The teacher sometimes finds him "zoned out" with a blank sheet of paper in front of him.

Arnold's IEP team evaluates the difference in language and instruction style in art class compared to other subjects where his grades are better. Observing class, they find that the instructor provides minimal detail in her directions. For example, she might say, "Get out your brushes and begin a portrait of someone you know." The teacher never describes what a finished portrait looks like, what line should be drawn first, or how to select a subject to paint.

Realizing that Arnold is struggling with the vagueness of the teacher's instructions, the team provides him with both verbal and written instructions that provide explicit, black-and-white steps and expectations. These guidelines explain how to begin a project, how to determine if and when it is complete, and what is and is not acceptable to turn in for credit.

The teacher begins writing the tasks and steps on the board and adjusts her language to be more direct and detailed. She also adjusts the schedule slightly to allow Arnold more time to prepare between projects. The teacher then gives him a cue five minutes before the current project is going to end.

As a result, Arnold begins turning in more projects at a higher percentage of completion and his grade improves. By addressing the issue early, the situation does not get out of control, and Arnold no longer approaches art class with anxiety driven by a lack of understanding of the teacher's expectations.

- Clearly define the first step or phase of a project.
- Avoid listing numerous steps or tasks at once without an assigned order in which to complete them.
- Explain what "finished" looks like and how to evaluate whether or not a project is complete.
- Offer additional processing time between tasks and when starting a new one.
- If a student becomes overwhelmed with open-ended choices, narrow it down to several options to choose from.

Chapter 4

Check-In Time
and Question Clarification

Social expectations can be challenging for students on the spectrum, not only with their peers but with their teachers as well. Open-ended rules or statements can be difficult for some students to interpret, resulting in the student feeling overwhelmed or frustrated. Even simple directions intended to help the student can have unintended consequences.

"Come to me if you have any questions." It's a common offer that accompanies many classroom projects. I had to take a moment to interpret those words every time I heard a teacher say them. I had to consider all of the possible meanings of that statement and how they related to me.

What kind of question can I ask? What if I am still perseverating on an issue from a project that happened days ago—is it too late to ask about it? What if I want to ask about something completely unrelated to the classroom project?

The teacher is speaking to another student, but I have a question. Is it okay to approach them now? If I wait too long, they will move on to another student and I will never get to ask my question.

No other student is getting up and walking to the teacher's desk. I don't want to be the first! Perhaps I misunderstood the instructions.

I processed the task slower than my peers, and now everyone has moved on, but I suddenly have a question. Is it okay to ask it now, or has the opportunity passed?

Some students hear, "Ask me if you have any questions," and think, *Oh boy, this is great because I have a lot of questions to ask! For example, why is the sky blue, and where do babies come from?*

When the teacher offers to answer any questions, without tying that direction to a specific project or area, the student may see it as a general classroom rule with no boundaries. Their honest interpretation of your words at face value can lead them to approach you at an inappropriate time, such as in the middle of a lecture, to ask an unrelated question. The student may misread you once and then never ask another question again for fear of repeating their mistake. Some students will look for opportunities to seek help without spotlighting themselves (the way they would by asking in front of the entire class), while others will only look for "raise your hand" opportunities and never seek one-on-one support. While there is no one approach that works for every student, there are several steps you can take that will make it easier for your students to understand the rules and know when and how to ask for help.

Using Clear Language

To support students who require clear instructions, first we have to change how we phrase the statement. We have to frame it in a way that is clear, leaves little room for interpretation, and gives the student defined boundaries.

Before the students begin work on the task, ask the group as a whole if anyone has any questions before they begin, then tell the students that if anyone has a question after that point, they can raise their hand (or come to your desk) and you will give them one-on-one assistance. You can also reword your offer. Rather than saying, "If you have any questions," try "If you are unsure what to do next…" or "If any part of this project is unclear…"

By offering a time for questions at the outset and then specifying what kinds of questions might arise, you are defining the area you are prepared to help with and making it very clear that your support at the moment is limited to the current task.

Make Your Availability Known

It's important to develop clear boundaries and structures outside of specific projects and integrate them into the general classroom environment. I often had trouble reading my teachers and determining, on any given day, when it was appropriate to approach them. Once I moved past elementary school, I had to learn to read many different teachers, and each one was approachable in a different way. Some preferred to chat after class, while others were in a rush to prepare for their next group of students and needed questions to be asked before the bell rang. Some teachers sat at their desk waiting for students to approach with questions, while others used the desk as a boundary that showed them to be inaccessible. Obviously, each teacher had their own system for supporting questions, but it was up to me to read them and determine what method each teacher wanted me to use.

To work around this, again, begin by framing everything clearly and issuing it as a classroom rule that is not specific to any one task. Also, consider this as part of a routine, so students can create one expectation and rely on that rule throughout the class or school year. If you change your availability on a regular basis, the student will question which method is appropriate at this time. Then the accommodation no longer removes their social anxiety.

The easiest way is to designate one time when you are available:

- "I will always stay after class for five minutes; you can come ask me a quick question before you leave."
- "I come back from lunch ten minutes early, so if you need to talk with me, just come back to the classroom before afternoon class begins."
- "I will be in the building for an extra thirty minutes after school ends every Friday afternoon. If you can't find time to talk with me during the week, you can always come to me with any questions or things you want to discuss after school on Fridays."

In each case, there is a daily or weekly routine that gives the student clear directions on when you are available and makes it clear that they can always fall back on that option if they miss other opportunities. It's a fail-safe.

Check-In Time

For students who need more one-on-one support or cannot determine when they need to come to you, you can add a specific check-in time. Just as with the last system, it needs to be a regular routine, but in this case it is initiated by you, not them. You can check in with the student every day at a specified time, such as before class or right as students leave for lunch. Or it could be a weekly meeting, where topics range from a quick "Are you okay?" to a ten- to thirty-minute window set aside just for that student. It may take time for the student to settle into the routine and learn how to take advantage of it. Establish the routine before expecting results; don't abandon your weekly meeting just because the student didn't ask questions the first few times you met.

No one system is going to fit everyone; the important thing is simply to develop a structured routine that lets the student know they will have your time and support, and when to expect it. Every time they think, *I am not sure how to do this,* or *I don't know what the teacher expects from me,* this routine diffuses the potential barriers with a simple answer: *But I can ask them at our next check-in time.*

For black-and-white thinkers who struggle with the social aspect of asking questions, try explaining it with examples. Ask a potential question such as "What page is the math assignment on?" or "What time are we having gym class tomorrow?" and then have the student tell you if that question is appropriate for the classroom or not. As an alternative, you can ask if the question falls into the category of "classroom" or "one-on-one meeting with the teacher." Some students may feel more comfortable with the option to answer on paper instead of verbally. In these cases you can write the questions on paper and let the student circle or mark which one is appropriate. You can also let them know whether a given question is appropriate for classroom discussion or should be saved for a private meeting.

For students who are less verbal or need a different method to ask for help, a nonverbal cue can also be effective. Provide the student with a token, such as a colored, laminated index card, and give them a system to use it as a beacon asking for help. The student can take the card out and put it on the corner of their desk or approach you and leave it on yours. In either case, it is a method for them to ask for your help, and to alert you to their needs, in a way that is both nonverbal and subtle. Some students may be comfortable asking for help in front of everyone, but others will appreciate the subtle nature of this simple communication tool.

Emily's Story

Emily had just started the third grade, and problems arose on the first day of school. She interrupted the teacher repeatedly during a lecture on classroom rules. Her questions had little to do with the topic and were very disruptive for the other students. Later in the day, she approached the teacher during a simple project and repeatedly asked what the lunch choices would be the next day. She ended the day standing at the teacher's side and asking so many questions about the next day's schedule that she nearly missed her bus.

To address these issues before they got out of hand, the teacher arranged for an after-school meeting the next day with Emily and her parents. After a brief discussion, Emily explained that the teacher had "said we could ask if we have any questions," and that is exactly what Emily had done. The teacher gave Emily a breakdown of the daily schedule and a printout of the weekly lunch menu to keep in her desk. Emily's parents took a copy of the lunch menu home so they could plan her meals on days when the cafeteria offerings did not meet her needs.

The teacher put in place a weekly check-in where Emily could ask questions and also explained what questions were appropriate to ask during class as opposed to during their one-on-one meetings.

Emily still asked questions out of turn from time to time, but her disruptive behavior decreased as she became accustomed to the schedule and got used to utilizing her one-on-one time to both discuss current projects and prepare for upcoming tasks.

QUESTIONS AND CHECK-IN TIME TIPS AT A GLANCE

- Structure your check-in time with the student as a regular routine that they can rely on. Be sure to give them notice if it is going to change.
- Prepare subtle options for students who are not comfortable raising their hand or calling out verbally for assistance.
- Rather than using open-ended statements such as "Ask me if you have a question," use specific and clear language, such as "If you are having trouble getting started…"
- Some students will need regular meetings, while others will do fine with a subtle nod of the head or a quick "How are you doing?" Not every accommodation has to feel formal.
- Remember that students on the spectrum are not intentionally monopolizing your time; they just need more explanation and support to understand boundaries.

Chapter 5

Social Rules

Social rules exist in every setting where there's a group of people. We observe these rules in the classroom, at the dinner table, and everywhere from conferences to cafes. Yet we rarely talk about these rules or explicitly state the boundaries that exist in group environments. We tend to agree on what is and is not acceptable within our culture without saying a word.

When you attend a class or seminar as an adult, the speaker rarely tells you that it's okay to get up and go to the bathroom. Or that you can borrow a pen from your neighbor if you want to take notes. They might remind you to silence your cell phone, but they don't tell you what to do if an emergency text comes in from your babysitter. Sometimes they don't even tell you if you can ask questions, or when it will be appropriate to do so. There are rarely instructions on how to choose a place to sit or a protocol if you arrive a few minutes late and need to find an empty chair in the back of the room.

Imagine how different that experience would be if those unspoken rules did not exist. What if you didn't know whether or not you could excuse yourself to take a call from the babysitter?

Or you didn't think it would be okay to get up and go to the bathroom halfway through the class? Even the most mundane elements of sitting in a roomful of people would cause anxiety. You would find yourself worrying about minor things. Everyone in the room would be tense.

This classroom environment is no different, and the unspoken rules grow more complex as the student ages. An elementary school teacher may spell out the rules and procedures all the way down to the proper way to ask for a bathroom pass, but by high school the students are generally expected to understand what is and is not acceptable without having it spelled out for them.

Social Anxiety on the Spectrum

It's important to look at the classroom environment with a fresh perspective that makes no assumptions. Consider all the little things you assume are acceptable, then imagine how the school day would feel if you didn't know the proper action to take unless it was explicitly stated by the teacher:

- *I ran out of paper. Is it okay to borrow some from a classmate? Do I have permission to ask them, or is talking against the rules?*
- *When is it okay to ask to go to the bathroom? Do I have to wait until the teacher is done lecturing, or until we are finished with our current project?*
- *The teacher told everyone to turn off their cell phones, but the student next to me is playing with his. What am I supposed to do?*
- *The schedule says we were supposed to start our next project five minutes ago, but the teacher hasn't told us to do so yet. Do I wait for their instruction or go ahead and start on my own?*

- *I'm late for class, and the teacher is already talking—is it okay to go in and find my seat, or will that disrupt the class?*
- *I always sit in the same spot, but today someone is already at my favorite desk. What do I do?*

Most of these questions are answered every day by making assumptions based on what people believe to be acceptable. Most people have never had a conversation about these scenarios, yet everybody makes a judgment and does what they think is appropriate. Students on the spectrum often struggle to make these judgments or need more guidance and explicit direction. We need to be told that it's okay to get up and go to the bathroom, or that it's okay to raise our hands if we have a question. Every student has their own perspective and ability to make these judgments based on their personal experiences, but explicit rules work for everyone.

Walk Through the Worst Case

When I work with a teen who has anxiety over seemingly minor issues, I like to start by talking through the situation from their perspective. I want to hear them explain what they are worried about and the possible outcomes that have them worried. Sometimes I continue that train of thought even further and we discuss the absolute worst-case scenario, which is often so unrealistic that it's funny. Then I ask them if that outcome is likely, and we discuss more likely outcomes. For example:

"I got to class late, and the teacher was already talking," said one of my mentoring students. "Everybody was in their seat, and I didn't know if I could go in and sit down or if that would interrupt the teacher."

"Well, let's say it did interrupt the lecture," I answered. "What do you think the teacher would do?"

"I don't know, maybe I would get in trouble."

"What kind of trouble? Would they kick you out of class? Give you detention? Send you to the principal's office?"

"I don't know, maybe," he said with a shrug.

"Have you ever seen another student come in late? What did the teacher do to them?"

"Yes, I have, and I didn't see the teacher do anything to them."

"Then I think you are probably okay walking in and sitting down, but I'd try to be quiet about it."

Instead of downplaying the student's concern, I want to talk through those concerns and get all the potential issues out in the open instead of percolating in the student's mind. My first goal is to hear them state what they are worried about and make it a tangible thing we can discuss instead of a vague, imagined worst-case scenario.

When I have a good rapport with the student, I may even talk through really silly and extreme cases to show them how easy it is to blow a minor thing out of proportion. I might say to the student in the example above, "The teacher might get so mad at you for interrupting his lecture that he tells you never to come back again. Then you are short one credit and have to take a whole extra year of high school to make it up, but by then all your friends have gone off to college and there are no scholarships left for you. Your only option is to apply for a job at a sandwich shop, but it's owned by the teacher's sister, and he's already told her all about you, so you don't get the job. You wind up living in a van down by the river. All because you were late to class one day. I can *totally* see that happening, can't you?" I give them a serious look for a moment, then I crack a smile and we laugh together at the fantasy of a life ruined by showing up late to class.

When you have these conversations with your students, talk openly about consequences and outcomes—don't leave it all to their imagination. Discuss what social faux pas look like and how they may be perceived by peers. Telling an off-color joke could offend another student, but eating lunch with a salad fork is unlikely to affect the student's social standing. I often tell my clients about social encounters I misread or mistakes I made. I joke about a pretty girl in a bar who seemed very interested in me right up until she introduced me to her boyfriend. I like to remind my clients that we all misread people from time to time—it's part of being human, and it's not the end of the world.

Maceo's Story

Maceo is a sophomore in high school. He does well in class and, while his social circle is limited, he gets along with his peers fairly well. His social interactions and demeanor are drastically different outside of the classroom. All of his social problems happen during lunch break, between classes, and before or after school. He has had issues scuffling with other students and misunderstandings that escalated into shouting matches.

The staff begins by looking at the environment where these issues occur. Within the classroom there is a clear social order, and the teachers define what is and is not acceptable. They provide an undisputable figure of authority. Outside of the classroom, this order vanishes, and there is often no oversight and no social structure at all.

By high school, many schools' social systems follow an old basketball saying: "No blood, no foul." If there is not a physical altercation, then nothing is wrong. Students on the spectrum often struggle in these open-ended environments where the social rules are constantly changing and are never stated up front. The same interaction can swing from appropriate to offensive when it moves into a different environment.

Maceo always greeted his teachers and support team with hugs when he was younger, and his few friends accepted it as part of his personality. No one has ever reframed that for him, but as a teen it is perceived much differently. When he sees his science lab partner at the lunch table, he walks up and greets her with a hug, which sparks a confrontation with her boyfriend.

Maceo needs support in understanding how the other students interact socially and how his habits or mannerisms may come across. Rather than teaching him that hugs are bad or that what he does is wrong, his support comes from context and explanation. The staff gives him some additional tools for how to greet his peers and offers some guidance on how to locate his friends at lunch, as well as on which situations to walk away from in the hallways.

With more understanding and a few new tools, Maceo adjusts his social interactions to avoid future problems and is better equipped to recognize bad situations and disengage before they escalate.

- Explain social rules clearly; do not assume the student intuitively understands what is and is not appropriate.
- Check in with the student about social encounters they've had outside the view of teachers and staff.
- Talk through social situations with the student after they occur. Ask questions and get a sense of the student's perspective to identify areas that need to be addressed.
- Clearly explains consequences, or lack thereof, to avoid unnecessary anxiety.
- Use real-life examples when teaching or discussing social skills.

SOCIAL RULES TIPS AT A GLANCE

Chapter 6

Routines and Schedules

Like most people on the spectrum, I want to live in an orderly world. I want to know what comes next and when the transition will occur, and I want clear warning well in advance of any changes to the schedule. Of course, those are not realistic expectations, but even as an independent and self-aware adult, my ideal schedule hasn't changed much since grade school.

In a perfect world, my school year would begin with a visual calendar that showed every single event that would break the normal routine. Every assembly, fire drill, field trip, or special event would be marked down so I could see it coming days or even weeks in advance. I might even color-code the schedule so I could clearly see every instance in which my normal routine would be disrupted. I would keep that calendar in the front of my binder or in my desk so I knew I could refer to it whenever I felt anxious about what might come next, or whenever I needed to reassure myself that the routine was not going to change.

Next, I would want a visual schedule that laid out the typical school day, hour by hour, and I would expect every day to follow that schedule unless it was specifically marked otherwise on the annual calendar. I would assume that my teacher was going to follow that schedule every single day and give advance notice of any changes.

These expectations may appear extreme, and you may think that it's impossible to please a student who wants things to function in this way, but there are several creative ways to make that student feel comfortable and prepared without creating unrealistic expectations.

Start by providing the schedule or agenda in multiple formats to ensure that it resonates with visual, auditory, and tactile learners. Post the schedule on the wall or board, describe it to the students, and also offer a physical copy that the student can carry with them.

Once the schedule is on display and the student has their copy, describe it aloud so the student can process it aurally and make them aware of common adjustments or instances where you expect to divert from the plan. Even a general reminder, such as "If we get a late start after lunch, we may go a bit longer on the afternoon project," will help those students adjust their expectations. Then encourage the student to mark their copy, take notes, or otherwise customize it to meet their needs. Remind them that they are in control and that copy is theirs to use however they need to.

Sample Schedules

There are many ways to design a schedule, and it does not have to be as rigid as a minute-by-minute daily plan. Here are several sample schedules written in different formats:

Schedule 1 (detailed):

9:00–9:10: Attendance and warm-up writing exercise
9:10–9:25: Lecture or instruction on today's project

9:25–9:40: Individual or group work time for today's project

9:40–9:45: Reflection and questions on today's project

9:45: Bell rings to signal next class

Schedule 2 (structured time blocks):

9:00–9:45: Morning activity #1

9:45–9:50: Questions, cleanup, and transition

9:50–10:30: Morning activity #2

10:30–10:40: Questions, cleanup, and transition

10:40–11:30: Morning activity #3

11:30–12:15: Lunch break

Schedule 3 (general items, no times or durations):

Turn in homework

Review and discuss textbook material

Lecture and worksheet

Short break

Group work time

Individual reading time

Recap and receive today's homework assignment

Schedule 4 (items with detail):

Morning journal: 10 minutes, writing on the topic of the day

Math review and questions: 15 minutes, reviewing yesterday's math assignment and asking questions about it

History textbook review: 45–60 minutes, reviewing chapter 4, discussion, and worksheet completion and turn in

Lunch break: 45 minutes

Art project: 30–40 minutes, painting or drawing a scene from the last book we read

While these schedules appear different and offer different levels of information, they all serve a similar purpose in that they:

- Inform the student of what is going to happen today, which reduces a large amount of anxiety that comes from wondering what is going to happen next.
- Give the student enough information to manage their own transition preparation.
- Help the student look ahead, allowing them to prepare questions in advance.
- Give the student a sense of control, since they know what will happen and they are not simply at the whim of the teacher.

Schedule #1 is perfect for a rigid classroom that follows the same routine every day. You could write the individual items next to each time block or print a standard schedule and have it displayed on the wall if you anticipate minimal changes. Post a notice near it if there are expected changes, as the student will develop a routine of looking to that location first and may be surprised and agitated if the change occurs without notice.

Schedule #2 maps the day out in time blocks and allows you to change the activity or task that fills each one while offering a consistent structure that will remain the same each day. This gives the student a good sense of what to expect while allowing you daily flexibility in how you order activities.

Schedule #3 offers the greatest freedom for the teacher and the least amount of information for the student. It is greatly helpful to order these items as you expect them to occur, to adjust the list if you change it during the day, and to check off each item as it is completed. This is a powerful support for visual thinkers. It enables them to prepare for what is coming while also seeing that the previous items have been checked off, which can support their transition between projects. Including small details such as breaks or question sessions can be helpful even if you are providing minimal details.

Schedule #4 requires more work on your part but gives the student all the information they need without being locked into the rigidity of schedules #1 and #2. You can reorder the items as needed and cross them off as with schedule #3. The student will feel less anxiety and experience smoother transitions with this system. If possible, give a printed copy of the schedule to the student at the start of the day, or consider offering it on days that are more chaotic and involve numerous transitions. Offering a physical copy is helpful even if the student is already familiar with the schedule.

If the student has a tablet or other technological support, consider assisting them in photographing the daily schedule as an alternative to providing a written copy. In either case, the purpose is not to duplicate the schedule you have posted on the board but to put them in control and give them some ownership of it. It allows them to refer to it even when not in the classroom, to take their own notes regarding it, or to go through the act of crossing items off by hand, which can be a powerful routine that helps them transition from one phase of the day to the next.

Even with strong systems in place, the student's schedule can be disrupted by events such as fire drills, tests, assemblies, field trips, or other special occasions. Whenever possible, give the student advance notice when changes are expected or special events are planned. Fire drills can be very stressful and disruptive for students who have sensory challenges and a need for rigid routine. Consider requesting advance notice of fire drills as part of the IEP or through coordination with the administration to ensure that the student is supported properly.

If your school uses multiple bells or alerts to tell students what time class starts and ends, make sure to provide that information to any student with auditory sensitivity. A card that says, "The bell rings five minutes before class begins, once when class begins, and once when class ends," will help them anticipate the sound and make it clear that there is a system and structure in place.

Kim's Story

Kim is in the first grade and struggling to follow the same pattern her peers do when they arrive in the classroom. The other students take out their homework, hang their jackets and backpacks in the closet, select their preferred lunch choice (hot meal, lunch from home, etc.) on the wall board, and then sit at their desks. Kim goes straight to the toy table at the back of the room, dropping her backpack and jacket on the floor along the way. She begins to play with her favorite toy train while the teacher asks her to take her seat. Some mornings require a long conversation before she will put the train down, and others end in a meltdown that effectively ends her day. She may hang her jacket one day, or mark the lunch board on another, but she never completes all the tasks that her peers do.

In evaluating her routine, the teacher finds that Kim doesn't perceive an order to the morning tasks and is oblivious to the fact that everyone else is following a set routine. The teacher maps out a very specific morning routine that details every item, in order, that Kim needs to complete upon arriving at class:

1. Take off backpack.
2. Take homework out of backpack.
3. Put homework on desk.
4. Hang backpack in closet.
5. Take off jacket.
6. Hang jacket in closet.
7. Select lunch choice from the board.
8. Return to desk.
9. Sit and wait for class to begin.

By detailing every step, the teacher gives Kim a clear routine to follow and does not leave anything off the list, no matter how minor it may be. It takes time for Kim to adjust to the routine, and the staff has to experiment with visual checklists that Kim can mark as she completes each task, but after a few weeks she gets comfortable with the system and is more successful in following the same routine as her peers.

Giving her a concrete plan removes the burden of observing and mimicking other students or trying to determine the correct order for her actions. Even if she understands that she needs to complete several tasks, the open-ended question of "Which one should I do first?" is a major stumbling block that is removed with a visual list provided by the teacher.

- Provide schedules visually, orally, and on paper for different kinds of learners.
- Notify the student about expected or possible changes to the normal classroom schedule or routine.
- Give the student advance notice of upcoming transitions.
- Allow the student control over their personal copy of the schedule.
- Help the student identify classroom routines and create a schedule for completing them.

Chapter 7

Sensory and Solo Options
for Group Projects

For many students on the spectrum, the words "group project" cause instant anxiety. Even a simple assignment can become overwhelming, and the knowledge that such a task is coming may cause daily stress even before the project begins.

Group projects usually break the student out of their normal routines, remove some of the tools and systems they normally use to self-regulate, and create a multitude of social challenges on top of the actual assignments. In my experience, I was often forced into a group with peers I didn't want to work with (and who didn't want to partner with me) or chosen last as a teammate because I was different and not in any of the social cliques. In either case, I was pushed into an uncomfortable social situation that removed most of my control and left me floundering to establish boundaries and a task list. Other students could use social cues or multitasking skills to decide on a course of action and find their role in the group, but I struggled mightily to find my place socially or within the project. I couldn't work at my own pace or tune out the din of the classroom to focus on my work. I had to read the other students, interpret their expectations of me, and try to match those against my own expectations for the project.

Even working with friendly, open-minded kids was a challenge for me. It was easy to become overwhelmed just by sitting at a table with several people, let alone doing so while working under a time constraint to complete a complex assignment. Group presentations were even worse, as my social anxiety was spotlighted in settings where everyone was supposed to present to the class.

In many cases I simply refused to participate. I would complete the project on my own, even if it took longer or reduced my grade, rather than deal with the social challenges and frustrations of partnering with a group of other students.

As I got older and developed friendships with some of my peers, I found that while I couldn't handle a full group, I could work one-on-one with a trusted partner. I once protested my placement in a larger group by exiting it with my close friend and doing our own project as a duo instead.

Managing Group Projects

There are ways to help students on the spectrum find success in groups. It starts with understanding their perspective and the potential issues that can hinder their ability to fully participate.

Students may mature at different paces or have greatly differing social experiences. Group placement should be considered, whether the students are selecting their own partners or are assigned partners by the instructor. Keep in mind, for example, that working with a group of girls may be a greater challenge for a teenage boy on the spectrum than it is for his male peers.

If the students are driving the pace of the project, it's important to match the student on the spectrum with peers who are more patient or are open to working at a slower pace.

Students on the spectrum may also need more clearly defined roles and boundaries, and choosing your words wisely will help.

The direction to "work as a team to make a collage that looks like a sailboat" sounds simple but is so open-ended that some of us won't even know where to start. You can make it clearer by defining who is going to get the supplies and which student will select the color of paper, or by giving the group a task list that shows all the steps involved, including discussion and decision making.

Options Instead of Opting Out

If group projects are challenging for the student, give them some options for getting out of the group if they cannot make it through the entire project:

- Give them one responsibility and allow them to exit after that aspect is complete. Or ask them to "assist" the group instead of being an equally responsible member.
- If the student cannot handle being in one group, give them a task to go from group to group as a helper, perhaps to share supplies or provide a specific direction or reminder. This keeps them engaged and part of the group, even if their role is different from that of their peers.
- Consider giving them a smaller group, either a duo with a friend or a small group that includes an aide or more mature partner.
- Offer an alternative location for the group to work in. Group projects often become noisy and overwhelming, especially with so many students talking at once in a small classroom. Allow this student's group to meet in the library, hallway, or another location that gives a reprieve from the din of classroom.

If the student cannot work in a group even with accommodations, then it's time to start a dialogue about what they would be willing to do, or what they would need in order to give it a try. It could begin with working one-on-one with a teacher or aide, or the student may have a specific strength they would like to showcase to their peers. If a student is more logical than artistic, it makes more sense to pair them up for a math assignment than an art project.

Relocation with Limits

Group projects are not the only cases where sensory input can become overwhelming and a student may need to relocate. Sometimes a student will need the option to work in a space that removes some sensory input. I found that I did my best on tests when I took them in the library instead of the classroom. Even when nobody was speaking, the sound of pencils on paper and the sense of all those bodies around me, stressed and anxious and focused on the test, were incredibly distracting.

You can choose one location such as the library, an alternate classroom, a hallway, or another area where the student would prefer to work when you can give them that option for certain projects. More mature students may want to take advantage of that option when they are stressed or feel extra anxiety over the project. Students who need more guidance can be offered the choice when the classroom is expected to be noisy or chaotic (students moving around) or when the test or project has high stakes and the student needs more processing power to focus.

Offering the option of the computer lab, or an alternate location where the student can use their own device, creates an easy solution as well. This provides the student with a place to work on their own, through a medium they are comfortable with, and doesn't single them out or force them from the classroom for negative reasons.

It's important to balance these options so the student is not isolated from their peers. Mainstreamed students on the spectrum often learn as much from the social experience as the academic lessons, so removing them from the group too often is not ideal. The key is to offer these options at the right times, to read the student, to judge when they will need options, and to give them as much control as possible. Sometimes just saying, "You can go to the library if you can't work in here," or "You can leave the group and work on your own if you are uncomfortable," is enough to help the student through the task because they know they are not locked in. The knowledge that they have an escape route is powerful even if they don't use it.

Ahmad's Story

Ahmad is a bright, attentive student in the fifth grade. He does well on most projects and does not have major behavioral issues. However, he struggles with group projects, and his participation is minimal, often ending with him shutting down, which not only ends his role in the group but negatively impacts his productivity for the rest of the day.

After several projects have all had similar results, the teacher observes that the next task is likely to cause another problem for Ahmad. The class is studying the original US territories, and students will break into groups, select one territory to study, and write a group report.

The teacher plans Ahmad's group before announcing that students can select their partners, guiding him to a smaller group with peers he knows. The teacher offers a few options for the group to select rather than leaving it open for discussion. Once the group has chosen a territory, the teacher tells them where to find that information in their textbook and how long they have to complete the project.

Ahmad is challenged by finding his role in the group, interpreting open-ended instructions, and identifying exactly what his responsibilities are. To assist him, the teacher talks with him before the project begins and gives him a list of his jobs for the project: contribute two ideas, say something positive about a peer's idea, and take responsibility for reading one page from the proper chapter in the textbook.

Lastly, the teacher recognizes that the room becomes much louder than normal during group projects. With students sitting in clusters, there is conversation in close proximity on all sides, which can overwhelm or distract Ahmad. The teacher suggests that his group move to a table in the library to work on their project. This allows Ahmad to focus on his role and responsibility without also facing an overwhelming sensory experience.

By giving him a clearly defined role, the right partners, and a more sensory-friendly environment, the teacher has given him all the tools he needs to be successful and engaged with his group. As Ahmad is typically engaged in the classroom, the teacher can also ask him about the experience later and fine-tune the accommodations for his next group project.

GROUP OPTIONS TIPS AT A GLANCE

- Offer a work space with less sensory stimulation during group projects or when the classroom environment is especially overstimulating.
- Allow the student to work with a single partner, smaller group, or alone instead of with a large peer group.
- Clearly define the student's role before they begin working with a group of peers.
- Don't force isolation; look for social interaction opportunities even when they push the student out of their comfort zone.

Chapter 8

The Power of the Homework Basket

Turning in assignments became progressively more difficult as I moved from grade school to high school. As classrooms became more crowded and each teacher went from managing 30 students to 150, it became my responsibility to turn my homework in. Each teacher had their own expectations and system for managing our assignments, and some teachers were accessible and flexible while others were indifferent and rigid.

I was a very fast typist, and I still communicate better via keyboard than pencil. Some teachers accepted my typed homework without question; others were so inflexible that even a request to use a pen instead of a pencil was seen as unreasonable. I had to learn not only how to fit my own abilities to each teacher's rules but how to interpret what they deemed acceptable. One teacher might accept a scrawled list of answers as a completed homework assignment while another might expect detailed notes showing the process. Some teachers would allow me to talk through the assignment or show my understanding verbally, and others would only grade based on what was on the paper.

An Unexpected Challenge: Turning in Homework

Reading and interpreting teachers' expectations was challenging, but the simple act of turning in homework was often a greater barrier. Even going back to grade school, I remember frustration and anxiety whenever we had to swap papers with a classmate to grade each other's work, or to pass our assignment to the front of the class. When I was stressed and anxious, or struggling socially with my peers, even that limited interaction was difficult. Now when I see a teacher ask their students to pass their homework to the front of the room, I still ask the same question I asked as a student: What happens if they don't?

The instruction itself to pass homework to the front of the room for collection leaves a lot of gray area.

Is this the only time that we can turn in that assignment?

What if I miss the prompt? Or I am late passing it in?

What if I'm not finished yet or, even worse, I miss the class entirely and never hear that prompt? Can I ever turn this assignment in, or was there only one window available to do so?

It may sound like a silly question, but some black-and-white thinkers will get stuck trying to figure it out or become anxious about the unknown outcomes and repercussions.

Fortunately, the solution is simple and easy to implement. All you need to do is standardize the process, maintain a routine (even if it's loose and not exactly the same each time), and provide the student with an "out" to avoid getting hung up on either anticipating or missing the prompt. The classrooms that worked best for me used at least one of the following systems, and my favorite teachers offered multiple options. Here are a few ideas:

- Provide a "homework basket" that has few boundaries. For example, declare that any assignment can be put in the basket any time, regardless of when it was due or how complete it is. You can spell out the grading system or simply state that an assignment that is turned in is always worth more than one that is not. Make sure this basket is located somewhere easily accessible and labeled clearly.

- Offer a regular routine for turning in late assignments or checking in to see what is overdue. You can make yourself accessible during a certain time every week or two, or schedule a specific time to go over the assignment list with the student to detail what they have not turned in. Offer to provide a written or typed list as well.

- Students in high school may require some one-on-one time to go through their binder or locker to find projects that have not been turned in yet. When I became overwhelmed, I would sometimes worry about turning in the wrong thing at the wrong time and hold on to it until it was too late. Sitting down with the teacher and going through my binder made it much easier to confirm what they wanted and to show them what I was holding on to.

I know that I still have a high school binder sitting on a shelf somewhere that contains assignments I completed but never turned in. The problem was not my ability to complete the task but the process of managing it and turning it in.

It can become overwhelming to keep track of so many projects spread out among different teachers, classes, timelines, and expectations. It may be unrealistic to expect each teacher to have the same system and accommodations, but if each teacher had offered some option for students like me, I know I would have found more success, especially in high school.

Li's Story

Li is a student in the sixth grade. Her grades are slipping in third-period math class. She is capable of doing the work but fails to turn in assignments and often arrives to class without her homework or textbook. While she doesn't often bring her math assignments with her to class, she always brings a brown paper bag with her and leaves it on her desk for the whole period.

Examining the situation more closely, Li's teacher realizes that the bag contains her lunch, which she brings from home each day, and math class is directly after lunch break. Other students arrive to class and immediately open their textbooks and take out their homework, ready to pass it forward as soon as the teacher asks for it. Li sits and waits, only to begin fishing for her assignment after everyone else has turned theirs in. She often stuffs it right back into her notebook as the class moves on from turning in homework to the day's assignment.

To evaluate her routine, the teacher looks at where Li is going before class. Her locker is at the other end of the building, and her classroom is near the cafeteria. Most days she does not walk the length of the building to put away her lunch bag and retrieve her math book from the locker; she goes straight from lunch to the classroom, carrying her leftover lunch in the bag with her.

She wants to follow the same routine as her peers, opening her textbook and then preparing to turn in homework, but without a textbook, she can't even get started. She's out of step with the rest of the class, stressed about being the only person in the room without a textbook and the only one with a lunch bag on their desk. By the time she works past the anxiety and finally takes her homework out of her binder, the rest of the class has moved on, leaving her lagging behind and unsure how to proceed.

To eliminate this issue, the teacher places a simple homework basket on his desk and tells all the students, including Li, that they can turn things in when they arrive or leave class, even if they miss the prompt at the beginning of class.

The IEP team also examines Li's schedule, required materials, and locker location. To simplify her routine and provide stronger supports, they suggest that her textbook and materials remain in the classroom so she does not have to fetch them from her locker. She is encouraged to leave lunch a few minutes early to make sure she has time to drop off her leftover lunch before class begins. Lastly, they inspect her daily schedule and offer her a new locker that is centrally located between her classes and easier to access on her way from the cafeteria to math class.

These simple accommodations lead to improved grades as well as less anxiety and frustration. Not only does she arrive to class prepared every day, she no longer brings her leftover lunch.

HOMEWORK BASKET TIPS AT A GLANCE

- Provide alternative systems for students who miss prompts to turn in homework.
- Check in with the student who is missing assignments or projects regularly. Don't let them fall so far behind that they become overwhelmed and give up.
- Give the student time to find completed assignments that may be lost in their locker or binder.
- Incorporate turning in homework into the daily routine and schedule.

Chapter 9

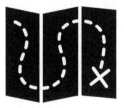

Transitions and Travel

Transitions during the school day were always challenging for me. I wondered when we would leave, where we would go, and what I should bring with me. Would the things I left behind be safe while I was gone? Would I be allowed to finish an incomplete project when we returned? Sometimes the thought of shifting from one project to another would create anxiety: *What if I don't finish in time?* Events that introduced unexpected transitions, from assemblies to fire drills, were jarring and overwhelming.

The sensory elements of moving from one classroom to another were also difficult. Even a small group of children moving together from the classroom to the library created an overwhelming amount of sensory input: the close proximity to them, the unintentional physical contact (as well as the elbow jabs and tripping that came from bullies), the echo of their shoes off the tile floor, and the chorus of conversation bouncing off the flat ceiling. Even keeping pace with a group of children could be difficult, especially when processing all the social and sensory stimulation.

I remember looking up at the red fire alarm bell in elementary school, always tense and ready to cover my ears should it suddenly go off. I was very sensitive to sound, especially sudden loud noises, and simply passing by the bell each day made me anxious.

As I got older the transitions became more complex and regular. In grade school we left the classroom a few times a week; in the higher grades, we were expected to move between several rooms each day. The shift into middle school was difficult, in part because the hallways were jammed with other students. The hallway wasn't just a way to get from one class to another; it was a social area where students gathered around their lockers to chat while they gathered materials or books for their next class. I couldn't work the combination lock or handle the press of bodies around me, and I began carrying every textbook to every class. The grade school bullies had also grown up, and my huge armload of books was a tempting target. The only thing worse than walking through those crowded hallways was stooping to gather my dropped books and assignments. I never wanted to arrive late, to walk in the door and have all those eyeballs staring at me, so I felt a great need to hurry through the crowded hallways to arrive before the bell rang.

My first attempt to solve the problem, by carrying all my possessions with me, only slowed me down and made me a target. My next attempt was to get a tape measure, a census, and a calculator. I wrote an article for the school newspaper to show my calculations for how many people were invading my personal space, as proof that the situation was unacceptable. My article was not published.

The Self-Advocate's Plan
After months of frustration and stress, something had to change. I created a plan. I would commandeer the desk nearest the door in every class, even those without assigned seating. I would watch the clock carefully, and five minutes before the class ended, I would quietly gather my things and leave. This gave me time to reach the

next class just before the bell rang and hundreds of students came pouring out into the hallway. Being the first one in meant I could claim my seat by the door without incident and continue my routine from class to class.

When I finally developed my own solution, I gave my teachers an ultimatum: do things my way or I will no longer attend your class. I didn't have IEP accommodations or much support from the staff, so I became a forceful self-advocate. Obviously, there are more proactive ways to implement accommodations, but I knew what wasn't working for me, I found a way to change it, and I fought tooth and nail to get what I needed to make it through the school day.

Looking back, I can analyze my system and examine the reasons it was successful for me:

- I never asked permission or allowed the teacher to single me out in front of the class.
- I was in control, and I determined when I would leave and how much time I needed to reach the next class. The teacher knew to support me should another student claim my desk, but otherwise they were passive and I was in charge. When I trusted a teacher, I would make sure to give them a nod or glance before I left, but otherwise it was a silent accommodation.
- I began keeping my textbooks in the classrooms instead of in my locker. My daily stress level was reduced once I no longer had to haul all those heavy books from class to class.

The system I used was a routine that was easily established and carried from class to class. Knowing that one part of my day would always be stable and in my control also reduced my anxiety and made it easier to get through the day.

Not only did I always arrive to class on time but I avoided the sensory and social chaos, the stress of trying to arrive on time, and the hallway encounters with bullies. It's not often that one accommodation can aid in so many areas, especially considering how little effort it took to implement (once the teachers accepted my system).

Mapping Transitions

While my transition system was helpful in middle school, high school was even more challenging in that the building was larger and my classes were more spread out than ever before. I had classes in entirely different buildings, or on different floors.

Being a visual thinker, I needed to experience the walk from class to class before I could navigate it during the actual school day. My first step was to take a list of my classes and physically walk from one to the next when the halls were empty. I could feel just how long the walk would take, consider whether or not I could stop by my seldom-used locker in between, and determine the fastest or least crowded route. Next, I printed out a map of the building and drew a line from each class to the next. I put this map in the front of my binder, next to my schedule, and it gave me a clear visual reference.

Students like me may do best with a visual reference, and it's best to provide it before their practice walk through the building. Use the following steps to make a powerful visual reference for or with the student:

- Print a map of the school's floor plan (these are often available to locate emergency exits). Make it as large as possible on a single sheet of paper so the student has plenty of room to write on it, or print it side by side with the student's daily schedule.

- Take a colored pen or pencil and draw a line connecting the first class of the day to the second class. This line should follow the same path through the hallways that the student will walk.
- Highlight the first class on their schedule with the same color, or write the class name, room number, and time in that color.
- Use a different color to repeat the process from their second to third class, matching each class and path with its own color.
- The line can include stops at the locker, restroom, or any other area the student needs to visit between classes.
- The same system should be used for all daily activities, including lunch break and study hall.

The end result should be a map with several colored lines, each tracing the path from one room to another, and a matching schedule that highlights each class with the color of the line.

For example:

9:00–10:00 a.m.: English, room #102 (red)
10:15–11:15 a.m.: Math, room #207 (blue)
11:15–12:00 p.m.: Lunch break, cafeteria (green)
12:00–1:00 p.m.: Art, room #115 (orange)

The following options may improve the effectiveness of this accommodation with some students:

- Color each classroom "box" on the map in with the same color as the line.
- Change the color of the line halfway between classes from

the first color to the second, showing the transition from one item to the next.

- Draw or highlight room numbers on the map if they are not included or easy to read.
- Help the student create the map themselves.
- If the student can't create the map and schedule, then let them select the colors and be present while filling them in. Some students with visual processing disorders may feel a strong need to choose their own colors.
- Add a list of required materials to the schedule and a note if they need to stop at their locker at set points throughout the day to pick anything up.
- Encourage the student to keep the map someplace easily accessible, such as in the cover or front of their binder. If the student needs more help keeping track of it, make multiple copies and/or laminate it.
- Check in with the student later to see if they find it helpful. Be flexible if they need to adjust their route or redraw things after finding their ideal path between classes.

For students who have challenges similar to the ones I faced, combining these two accommodations—walking the route for practice and mapping it out for reference—can make a huge difference, especially in middle and high school. It's important to implement these strategies early to assist the student in learning the layout of the new building as well as their class schedule. Give the student as much control as possible, from choosing the colors to deciding what type of schedule and notes suits them best. It can be on a single sheet or have one page with the map and a second with the schedule, either in black and white or color coded.

The transition to a new school, grade, or schedule is already going to be a challenge for some students. Use visual supports not only as a day-to-day accommodation but as a resource to help the student transition into their new schedule, especially if the previous school or grade required less travel and transition. The time you spend before school starts, or in the first week, will pay off for the rest of the year.

James's Story

James is fourteen years old and a freshman in high school. The larger campus is challenging and overwhelming, so he often arrives to class late and agitated. Teachers have let it slide when he is tardy, but nothing has improved, and he has recently begun reporting confrontations with other students between classes.

His support team meets to arrange a walk-through of the building after the school day ends. A friend walks with James from class to class in the empty building, and a staff member suggests the best path from one area to another. The team also provides him with a printed map of the school and colored markers so he has the option to trace or draw his route and he can choose to color code the system as well.

Teachers also offer him the choice to sit near the exit and the freedom to leave each class a few minutes early to begin his commute before the bell rings. Analyzing his path, they realize that his locker is far from most of his classes and he returns to it regularly to retrieve textbooks and other required items. To reduce his travel time and anxiety, teachers allow him to keep his textbooks and other materials in the classrooms to reduce trips to his locker and the number of items he has to carry between classes.

After these accommodations have been implemented and James has been given time to adjust, he arrives to class on time with less anxiety, and his reported hallway incidents also decrease.

TRANSITIONS TIPS AT A GLANCE

- Offer a printed map of the building and mark the rooms and hallways the student will travel through.
- Allow the student to walk through the building outside of normal school hours to experience the path from class to class in empty hallways.
- Give the student more time to get from one location to another.
- Minimize the amount of materials the student needs to carry between classes.

Chapter 10

Meltdowns and Overload

The word "meltdown" is used often, though it means different things for different students. For some, a meltdown is a full tantrum with tears and clenched fists. Others may have an outburst and flee. You may meet some students who have the opposite reaction and simply shut down, refusing to communicate, participate, or interact at all. Every student is different, with their own triggers, thresholds, and reactions, but there are some common elements that affect most people on the spectrum.

Meltdowns or severe behaviors are not always caused by the "trigger" or setting event—rather, they are often a culmination of multiple issues compounded by the student's processing differences. You may find that "meltdown" describes the final outburst but "overload" is what you are actually witnessing.

The school environment offers very few escapes from sensory and social input. Even if we are between projects and not actively contemplating an academic task, we are still in an environment that is usually bright, noisy, social, and at least somewhat unpredictable. Many of us on the spectrum struggle to let things go, and students can perseverate on a missed cue, a wrong answer, or something as minor as the sensory experience of another student bumping into them in the hallway. Students on the spectrum are trying to juggle all the little things that are more difficult for them than for their peers while managing the academic responsibilities of being a student and expending much of their processing power on sensory and social challenges. Finally, they reach a point where they are maxed out and can no longer function. Something sets them off, and they melt down or shut down, even if the instigating event seems minor. It may even seem as if they went off at random and there was nothing to trigger the meltdown.

Picture a kettle full of water. If you leave it on the stove for long enough, the pressure will build up and it will boil over. The hotter the stove, the faster it boils. The only solution is to reduce the heat and be prepared to take it off the burner before it reaches the point of no return. Our brains are similar: they can only handle so much. The "heat" and accompanying pressure is caused by everything we experience: trying to grasp long division, pondering the tone of a peer's voice, feeling the weight of two coins in a pocket, or hearing the sound of them clinking together. All of this data requires energy and effort to process.

When we try to process social cues, sensory overload, and multiple intellectual tasks at once, we simply run out of processing power and can no longer function. When I get to that place, I can feel it building. Knowing I am almost maxed out causes even more stress, especially if I don't see any way to stop it. Even if I take a deep breath and set aside the project I am working on, my mind is still processing the sensory world around me and may be stuck on previous tasks or experiences that I have not moved on from yet. A student sitting in a noisy classroom and processing light, sound, voices, and academic tasks may be overloaded. Telling him to take a break from his assignment may reduce the academic pressure, but it does not address all of the other things that are happening simultaneously.

Providing an escape from one area may leave the others simmering, building toward a meltdown despite your efforts to give the student a break.

Turning Down the Heat

The first step in managing overload is to give breaks that allow the student an escape from different areas of stress as well as a plan that helps them cool down. When I was a child, the common "accommodation" was to send me to the front office if I was misbehaving or uncomfortable in the classroom. I went from a bright, noisy, chaotic environment to a different bright, noisy, chaotic environment. There, instead of processing my peers' behavior and our academic projects, I had to process the phone ringing, questions from the staff, and people coming and going all around me. How could I possibly calm down? Every kid who walked by asked, "What did you do to get sent to the office?" Even though this was meant as a support, it often had the opposite effect.

I knew something had to change, so I developed my own plan. There was a dark, quiet stairwell that was not used often and was located on the side of the building away from most of the classrooms and students. I felt safe and comfortable there, and it became my go-to location when I needed to get away. I thought of it as my safety valve, a place I could go to in an emergency. The stairwell was an escape from both sensory and social processing, allowing me to calm down and process the issues I was working through. I would return to the classroom closer to my baseline, further from my boiling point. As I got older I discovered the library and computer lab were other quiet, safe spaces that provided a respite from the overstimulating classroom environment, and it was easier to request taking a test in the library or working in the computer lab than to wait until I was maxed out and had to flee to the stairwell.

When you look for a location that supports the student's sensory needs, start by evaluating the environment as a whole and remember that the student may have some hypersensitivities. A quiet room is great—unless there is a flickering fluorescent light. A table in the hallway near a window might have calming natural light—and a steady stream of other kids walking by while your student attempts to focus. I often found it calming to walk a lap around the school or pace the halls, but that accommodation was not effective if other students or staff stopped to chat with me. Each student is different, and knowing their individual needs will help you identify potential triggers that may rule out a location as an appropriate safe space.

At a calm moment, ask the student where they are most comfortable or where they would like to go when they need to take a break. Some may want to sit quietly in the library to get away from the classroom; others may process best by walking the halls or pacing in the empty gym, as the act of walking or pacing can be a self-regulation tool that helps the student process and get back to their baseline. Some students will need a quiet space where they can go to work on assignments, but others will need that quiet space to be task-free, where they can invest all their energy in calming down without trying to simultaneously work on an academic task.

Sometimes you will have to use the location as a way to remove one type of input to focus on another. For example, the classroom may be too loud and busy for the student to engage in a group project, but if you send their entire work group to the library, the student can focus better on socially engaging with their peers. At another time they may need to go to an empty room, with no social engagement at all, to focus on taking a test or completing a project.

You can look for times that make an area more appealing, such as using the empty classroom while other students are at lunch or in another part of the school. There may be certain hours when the gym, library, or other spaces are always open, and those times can become part of the student's routine, or an option they can choose to take advantage of when they need to.

Improving Methods

An escape from sensory input can be a great tool but, as with any accommodation, it can also be used improperly. When I was in the sixth grade, I was having regular meltdowns, running from class, leaving the building, or getting into physical altercations with students and staff.

On several occasions I was literally carried into the special ed room and forced into a closet space that was no more than six feet long and narrow enough that I could stand in the center and place my palms on either wall. The heavy wooden door had a plastic window that was covered with construction paper on the outside, and the door was locked once I was alone in the room.

I yelled, screamed, beat on the window, kicked the door, and every now and then, the corner of the paper would peel back and a pair of eyes would peek in at me before they retreated and the paper was taped back down. I had no sense of time during my experience in that room, and instead of calming down, I became even more agitated and furious. By forcing me into this room, school staff removed my ability to process on my own terms, took away all of my control, and offered no resolution or answers to whatever issues had set me off in the first place.

Fortunately, that practice is not so common today, and in many places it is illegal. Even so, it is a reminder that something may meet all of our requirements (quiet, dim, no social interaction, ample processing time) and still be inappropriate. The strongest element we have to offer is control, because giving the student more control over their environment, or the circumstances that led them into a meltdown, can be more powerful than the environment itself.

Helping the Student Find a Safe Space

There are many ways to empower a student to access their "safety valve" location. Some students have the tools to identify their need to get away, and they can be trusted to go there on their own. Others may need to raise their hand, display a card, or use a nonverbal cue to alert you of their need to get away before they have a meltdown.

There is no one system that works for everyone, so it is best to start with a dialogue and ask the student what their preference is or offer several options for them to choose from. It can also help to show flexibility and let them know that if this location or method does not work, it's easy to change and they are not locked in once they agree to one system. You may implement the system by having them raise their hand and ask to be excused when they need to go to the library, but if that fails, you can give them an emergency hall pass to keep in their desk instead, allowing them to go for a walk or to their "safety valve" location without a prompt from you. The student is more likely to buy in and try the accommodation if you reduce the stakes and make it clear that you are flexible and willing to try different options until you find the way that works best for them.

Sam's Story

Sam is a student in the second grade, and even though he has an IEP and classroom accommodations, he sometimes has meltdowns that result in a number of behaviors, including shouting, throwing things, and slapping at staff and other students. When he is not melting down, he is usually a good participant in projects and has shown the capacity to function in a standard classroom environment.

Meltdowns are challenging because there is no one solution, and it often takes a team effort to identify the right accommodations. His IEP team has to work together to explore every possible contributing factor, from sensory overload to whether or not he ate breakfast on the day of an outburst.

The team implements a "safety valve" option, allowing Sam to request a walk around the building with an aide to help him regulate and get back down to his baseline. The aide and teacher also have the option to suggest a walk if they see him getting agitated.

The behavior may require a more detailed plan than his teacher is equipped to provide, so the team discusses a full Functional Behavior Assessment and Behavior Support Plan to create the strongest accommodations specific to his needs.

While his teacher may not have a single solution that solves the problem, she can support him with the option to go for a walk when needed, suggest it when she sees him nearing his breaking point, and offer additional breaks between tasks or a reduced assignment load while the team works to build a more thorough and individualized approach.

- Give the student a way to leave the room if they become overstimulated.
- Provide breaks from sensory and social stimulation.
- Don't analyze meltdowns only by the events immediately preceding them; look at the big picture.
- Offer the student an alternate environment to work in when they need to focus or have become overstimulated by the classroom.
- Implement a "safety valve" for students who have meltdowns or become overstimulated.

OVERLOAD TIPS AT A GLANCE

Chapter 11

Mentoring

Students with disabilities or processing disorders often suffer from low self-esteem, and older students may have a history of negative experiences in school. Some students are used to lagging behind their peers, and as they get older, failure and struggle may become such a routine that the students expect them. A long history of failure may lead even teachers and parents to see it as inevitable, which can have a long-lasting impact on the student. We become used to falling behind, complacent with the feeling that everyone around us is more capable and successful. Everyone else gets an opportunity to shine, to showcase their ability, to be the expert. But those opportunities are less common for students on the spectrum, especially those who have never found consistent success in the classroom.

Everyone deserves an opportunity to share their strengths, to lead, and to receive genuine positive feedback from their peers. Even for those who are positive and well prepared for success, it's still important to find opportunities to flip the script and provide opportunities to lead others.

It sounds backward: if you have to change and adapt your class-room to accommodate a student who would otherwise struggle, how can you possibly expect that student to also take on a leadership role? The answer is different for each student, but even heavily impacted individuals can be guides to others if offered the proper opportunity.

Many people on the spectrum have a passion or focus; some people may call it an obsession. I've met young people with a great knowledge of one topic or area: math, video games, books, languages, history, geography, art, etc. Learning about a student's passion gives you a blueprint for how to shift them into a different role. If a student has a passion for one subject, such as history, they can be given the opportunity to lead a small group in a class project or invited to share their expertise on a relevant topic with the class. You can also give these students the opportunity to help others who are struggling with the subject or need some additional support. If there are students who are having trouble grasping a math concept, then the student on the spectrum with the passion for mathematics may be a great addition to that particular work group.

It's important not to make knowledge a punishment. I had my first computer before I was two years old, and I grew up in a household full of computers and technology. When I began high school, we had a mandatory typing class. As my peers struggled through the daily typing tests, I was typing over eighty words per minute. The teacher "accommodated" me by requiring that I complete every assignment twice. Even then, I finished quickly.

I discovered that my peers were impressed by my speed and comfort with computers. They began asking me to spend my extra class time typing their projects for them. Even the nasty bullies saw me as valuable when my typing skills earned them extra credit for turning in neatly formatted assignments. My reward for recognizing my area of strength and leveraging it to improve my social status in the classroom: I was suspended from school for cheating by typing other students' work. Not only did they punish me twice for being good at something, but they took away my greatest strength at the time when it was my best opportunity to connect with my peers.

Mentoring and Being Mentored

Mentorship does not require a student to be particularly good or skilled. The social experience of being a leader or guide is valuable whether the student is an expert or a novice. Most people have a positive feeling when others look to them for help or seek them out to assist in solving a problem or overcoming a barrier. Yet this experience is often denied to students who need extra support.

In middle school, I connected with one teacher and did well in his class, so I signed up as his assistant for the following term. Many of the students in that class were in the same grade as me, but they came to me for help. My tasks were minor, but it felt good to sit in the back of the room and know what joke the teacher would tell next, or the surprise ending he had planned for a quirky project. Those experiences gave me something valuable that was not common during my time in school.

Acting as a teacher's assistant can be beneficial for students at any grade level, though you may find more opportunities for students to take on such roles in middle and high school, where they will have several teachers and shorter classes. Having numerous classes each day means the student will experience many different teaching styles and classroom environments. The shorter class lengths will make it easier for the student to assist without becoming overwhelmed.

Don't push the idea of assisting immediately; allow the student some time to get comfortable with their routine and classes before suggesting the idea of assisting in a class. I like to start with a conversation about their favorite teachers and what makes those classes enjoyable; the positive discussion makes for a natural segue to the idea of helping out or repeating the class during next semester as an assistant.

Once the student is paired with a teacher they connect with, the specifics of their role can be adjusted based on the student's needs and ability. If you have a student assisting you, be creative and flexible in the tasks and responsibilities you give them. One of the great benefits of mentorship is the social opportunities it affords, as even such minor tasks as checking in with students during a group project or passing out or collecting materials can create positive social experiences. Consider the following as ideal experiences and outcomes for students who act as teacher's assistants:

- Experience handling new and varied responsibilities
- Opportunities to connect socially with peers
- Participation in group activities with a distinctive role
- Greater confidence and self-esteem built by partnership with the teacher

Finding Ways to Lead

For students with more significant challenges, there are still many opportunities to guide others. Sometimes the answer is as simple as helping younger children and leading by being the oldest in the room. A student may struggle with their coordination and be the worst basketball shooter in fifth-grade PE class; move that same student into a leadership role with the second-grade PE class, and you may see a whole different side to them. Even if their actual task is as simple as retrieving the basketballs or guiding those younger students to line up in the right place and take turns shooting the ball, that student is going to feel confident in ways that they do not when participating in the fifth-grade class.

If you move that student into a support role among their peers, you are singling them out as different, saying, "You are no good at shooting the basketball, and it's obvious, so just pick up the ball for the other students instead." That undermines the student and cuts even deeper into their self-confidence. If you take them to the younger students and introduce them as a guide, then the task may be the same, but the explanation is different: "You know the rules and the plan better than any of these kids do. You are my helper, and your job is to guide these kids and allow them to come to you for help. If you don't know what to do, then you can bring the matter to me."

School is hard, especially when you know that you are different and you can see your peers moving easily in areas where you struggle. Watching all those kids talk at lunch, making friends and developing meaningful social connections, can be painful when it's a great mystery to you. It's like watching others converse easily in a different language while you can only make out a few words here and there. Over time it can grow into acceptance. *I will always be last, so my goal is never going to be higher than last place because I know I'm not capable of more. I am always the one asking for help or the one the teacher singles out because he knows I need more help, so I will expect to always be behind my peers.* That thinking may not be visible from the outside, but it is not uncommon among students on the spectrum, and it may be deeply ingrained by the time some of them reach middle or high school.

Mentoring is not about giving someone an artificial sense of power or competence. The goal is not to create a false environment where a student appears to help others who do not really need their help. My goal is always to lift others up and give them the opportunity to help, to provide the tools and opportunity to be a leader, even if that means knowing when to ask the teacher for help.

Supporting Leadership (and Swordsmanship)

I teach a workshop with "boffers," which are handmade foam replicas of medieval weapons. We build swords, shields, axes, and all manner of weapons. The majority of my participants are on the spectrum, verbal, and between the ages of twelve and twenty-four. After they are familiar with the rules and equipment we use, I break them into groups.

We form a huddle, like a football team, and I take the lead. I point across the field to the other huddle, then I single out the quietest, meekest student in my group. I ask them if they have any ideas on how to approach the coming battle. Can they recommend a strategy or specific tactic our team should use? If they do, then I give them the floor and make sure everyone on the team listens to their plan. If they need more support, I narrow the question down into a multiple-choice scenario: "John is over there on the other side, and he's probably their best fighter, plus he has that really big sword. Do you think we should all team up to take him out first, or should we avoid him and try to beat their weaker players before focusing on him?" I frame the question directly to that student, but I include the whole group and make sure that my request for a strategy recommendation is sincere.

If my student proposes an unwise strategy, I have two choices: I can support it and let the group follow them, and if it fails, we can learn from it and discuss a counterstrategy for the next round. Or I can use positive wording to offer an alternative: "I like your idea of splitting up, but the other team might stick together and pick us off one by one. What if we split up at the beginning just like you said, but once they cross the middle of the field, you call everyone back together? Your team will wait for your signal, so be sure to call it out loud so they know when to come back to you."

I've seen students come out of their shell and become leaders once I, as their teacher, defer to them and offer them a chance to address the team. I've seen others who don't have the skills to propose a strategy, but when I, as their leader, ask for that student's input or approval, their demeanor changes. The teacher is asking them for advice, or asking for their "okay," before moving ahead with the plan.

How often do any of us get to approve the teacher's lesson plan before it moves forward? Imagine how you would feel if your own teacher gave you that opportunity, and in front of the whole class!

Jonathan's Story

Jonathan is a student in the fourth grade. He's intelligent and capable but struggles to connect socially with his peers and becomes overwhelmed in high-sensory environments and by fast-paced transitions. He enjoys music class, but the lack of a standard routine is hard for him and the open-ended expectations of the class also cause problems.

His music teacher offers him the opportunity to assist with the second-grade recorder class. He doesn't know anything about the recorder (and later, after sixteen years in the music industry, *still* has no idea how to play the recorder), but he is tasked with handing out sheet music and instructing students in proper posture and technique: shoulders back, elbows in! Being two years older than the students and declared an assistant by the teacher puts him in a leadership role despite his lack of skill with the instrument itself.

Instead of removing him from the music program entirely, the teacher changed his role and created clear expectations for him to follow. The benefit is not in learning the art of the recorder but in guiding other students, being part of the group, and connecting socially from a position of strength. Not only does it keep him involved in the music program but it leads to other opportunities to assist teachers and builds a routine that continues for years afterward. He learns how to help, when to ask for help, and how to make himself available as a leader or assistant for others.

He never learns how to play the recorder, but twenty-five years later, he continues to guide others and assist teachers.

- Let the student shine during projects and subjects that match their strongest skills or area of interest.
- Put the student in a leadership role assisting younger peers.
- Encourage students in middle and high school to become a teacher's assistant. Wait until after the first semester to pair them with a teacher they are familiar with.
- Take advantage of leadership opportunities, even if they are brief and temporary.
- Remember that mentorship can teach social skills and does not need to be driven by academic ability.

Everyday Advocacy:

The Ultimate Goal

I'm often asked if my experience in school was really similar to the experience of students I work with today. People see me as a capable, social adult who seems worlds apart from the overwhelmed, struggling students in today's classrooms. I understand why people see me speak at conferences and have trouble picturing me as a child so out of control that the staff saw the need to literally lock me in a closet. To some, it seems unlikely that someone could really struggle so much in school and go on to find a healthy, happy life in adulthood.

The truth is that I have come a long way from where I was as a student, and it's not because I'm special, talented, or more capable than my peers. What set me apart was a self-awareness that matured at a young age, along with a great amount of something between stubbornness and determination. I taught myself to be a self-advocate and pushed myself constantly, sometimes to prove others wrong but more often to prove to myself that I could realize the reality I saw in my mind and that I didn't have to rely on others to create it for me.

A teacher at a conference recently asked me if their students on the spectrum would really look like me and advocate for themselves like I did. The answer is no, most students won't advocate as clearly and bluntly as I did, and very few will present themselves to you at twelve years old in the same way I present myself in my thirties. That's not to say they will not get there, but it takes work and experience that doesn't happen overnight. But you will meet students like me: children who have potential and need the right environment to bring it out, who are capable but struggling to fit in, and who will surely surprise you when given the chance.

I can't speak for everyone on the autism spectrum, and I don't claim that every tool in this book will be the perfect fit for each student you meet. The autism spectrum is as vast and varied as the rest of humanity. You will also find students who do not have an autism diagnosis but will benefit greatly from the accommodations described here. In the end, the labels don't really matter. What's truly important is creating an environment that works for everyone and provides the right supports for different thinkers.

These accommodations I have described are just first steps. It's up to you to tailor them to your students, stretch them to fit your classroom, and evolve them over time. I look forward to hearing from you and learning how you have adapted these tools to fit your classroom and your own improvements on my concepts. I would love to hear stories of your students who utilized accommodations to reach their goals.

Ultimately, the most powerful tools available are not well-written IEPs or a masterful classroom rule sheet. They are understanding, empathy, and the ability to set your assumptions and judgments aside to view things through your student's eyes. I hope this book has helped you to better understand how things look through the eyes of a student on the spectrum and some of the ways we see and think differently than our peers.

I believe that the goal of accommodations is to empower young people to reach their potential with the same opportunities as their peers. Every support is there to lift them up, not to limit their options, to help the student navigate and overcome their challenges, not to mask them or help the student avoid the things they struggle with. Most importantly, every accommodation is the opportunity to put control into the student's hands and allow them to learn self-advocacy skills through experience. When we raise expectations and empower the student to take control, we are not just teaching a skill or helping them get through that day's activity. We are preparing them for life after school with self-advocacy tools that they will use every day.

More from the Author

I work in Portland, Oregon, but I travel throughout the country as a speaker. I am available for events large and small, offering presentations on classroom accommodations, transitions, independence, and the inner workings of the autistic mind. I enjoy meeting teachers and traveling to schools or universities to teach about accommodations and understanding autism.

You can visit me at www.JonathanChase.net to learn more about my mentoring services and presentations (and hear some of my original jazz compositions as well). I also have a number of interviews, articles, and videos spread across the Internet. A quick search of my name will also bring up my TED Talk, "Music as a Window into the Autistic Mind."

Feel free to write to me. I would love to hear what works for your students and how these accommodations have changed your classroom. I'm happy to answer questions, speak to students or family members, and discuss my services as a speaker and consultant.

CPSIA information can be obtained
at www.ICGtesting.com
Printed in the USA
LVHW041411150123
737212LV00014B/584